EVERYTHING YOU NEED TO KNOW ABOUT

HARRY STYLES

Welcome to *Everything You Need to Know About Harry Styles*, the ultimate guide to Harry's meteoric rise to fame. From the early days of *The X Factor* and the unexpected formation of One Direction, to his remarkably versatile media career, we share the heady highs of Harry's life, peppered with some fun facts and little-known tidbits about the man himself.

Not only do we explore Harry's musical career – including how One Direction became unexpected global superstars thanks to their devoted fans, and how Harry made it on his own after the band's hiatus – we delve into Harry's evolution from teenage heart-throb to star of the silver screen and certified fashion icon. Jam-packed with over 140 incredible pictures, you'll get to know the man himself inside and out!

FUTURE

FUTURE

EVERYTHING YOU NEED TO KNOW ABOUT

HARRY STYLES

Future PLC Quay House, The Ambury, Bath, BA1 1UA

Editorial
Author **Sophie Barton**
Group Editor **Philippa Grafton**
Senior Designer **Perry Wardell-Wicks**
Senior Art Editor **Andy Downes**
Head of Art & Design **Greg Whitaker**
Editorial Director **Jon White**

Cover images
Getty images

Photography
All copyrights and trademarks are recognised and respected

Advertising
Media packs are available on request
Commercial Director **Clare Dove**

International
Head of Print Licensing **Rachel Shaw**
licensing@futurenet.com
www.futurecontenthub.com

Circulation
Head of Newstrade **Tim Mathers**

Production
Head of Production **Mark Constance**
Production Project Manager **Matthew Eglinton**
Advertising Production Manager **Joanne Crosby**
Digital Editions Controller **Jason Hudson**
Production Managers **Keely Miller, Nola Cokely,
Vivienne Calvert, Fran Twentyman**

Printed in the UK

Distributed by Marketforce, 5 Churchill Place, Canary Wharf, London, E14 5HU
www.marketforce.co.uk Tel: 0203 787 9001

Everything You Need To Know About Harry Styles First Edition (MUB4793)
© 2022 Future Publishing Limited

FUTURE Connectors.
Creators.
Experience
Makers.

Future plc is a public
company quoted on the
London Stock Exchange
(symbol: FUTR)
www.futureplc.com

Chief Executive **Zillah Byng-Thorne**
Non-Executive Chairman **Richard Huntingford**
Chief Financial and Strategy Officer **Penny Ladkin-Brand**

Tel +44 (0)1225 442 244

Widely
Recycled

ipso. For press freedom
with responsibility

CONTENTS

THE X FAC

HOW THE TEENAGE HARRY WENT FROM BAKER BOY TO POP SENSATION

TOR

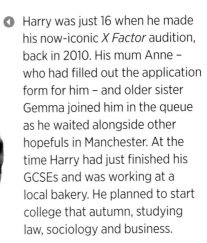

Harry was just 16 when he made his now-iconic *X Factor* audition, back in 2010. His mum Anne – who had filled out the application form for him – and older sister Gemma joined him in the queue as he waited alongside other hopefuls in Manchester. At the time Harry had just finished his GCSEs and was working at a local bakery. He planned to start college that autumn, studying law, sociology and business.

Image: FilmMagic / Getty images

HARRY HAD JUST FINISHED HIS GCSES AND PLANNED TO START COLLEGE THAT AUTUMN, STUDYING LAW, SOCIOLOGY AND BUSINESS

Harry was thrilled when the judges put him through to the next round, but victory turned to crushing defeat when he failed to make it through the Bootcamp stage. Devastated, he was set to return home when he was recalled, alongside other soloists Niall Horan, Liam Payne, Zayn Malik and Louis Tomlinson. It emerged the judges had a proposition – did they want to form a boyband, keeping them in the running? The answer, of course, was yes.

Image: Danny Martindale / FilmMagic / Getty images

A nervous-looking Harry famously sang Stevie Wonder's hit 'Isn't She Lovely' for *The X Factor* judging panel. "I'm in a band," the cheeky, Cheshire-based teenager told host Dermot O'Leary, adding that he was the lead singer for White Eskimo, a group he'd formed with his school friends. They had recently won a Battle of the Bands contest, giving Harry a taste for fame. "I got such a thrill when I was in front of people singing," he revealed.

Image: Simon Harris/SH Photography/
Contour by Getty Images

Did you know?

AS SOON AS THE BOYBAND WAS FORMED, THEY FACED THE DAUNTING TASK OF COMING UP WITH A NAME – AND THEY NEEDED A MONIKER THAT WOULD BE WORTHY OF SUPERSTARDOM. MANY FANS ASSUMED IT WAS SIMON COWELL WHO CALLED THE GROUP 'ONE DIRECTION', BUT HARRY LATER REVEALED THAT IT WAS IN FACT HIM WHO SUGGESTED THE NAME. "I THOUGHT IT SOUNDED GOOD," HE SAID. "WE THREW AROUND NAMES FOR A LITTLE BIT, AND I HONESTLY DON'T KNOW. I SUGGESTED IT AND EVERYONE WAS LIKE 'YEAH WE LIKE THAT' AND THEN IT KIND OF STUCK, AND THAT WAS WHAT IT WAS."

Longing for a shot at stardom, Harry and the boys set out to impress the *X Factor* judges, Cheryl Cole, Louis Walsh, Dannii Minogue and Simon Cowell. Their competitors included singer and songwriter Matt Cardle – the show's eventual winner – runner-up Rebecca Ferguson, Cher Lloyd, Wagner, Mary Byrne and Katie Waissel. Aged between 16 and 18, the boys were among the youngest competitors on the show – but they were also among the most talented.

Image: Dave M. Benett / Getty Images

THE BOYS WERE AMONG THE YOUNGEST COMPETITORS ON THE SHOW — BUT THEY WERE ALSO AMONG THE MOST TALENTED

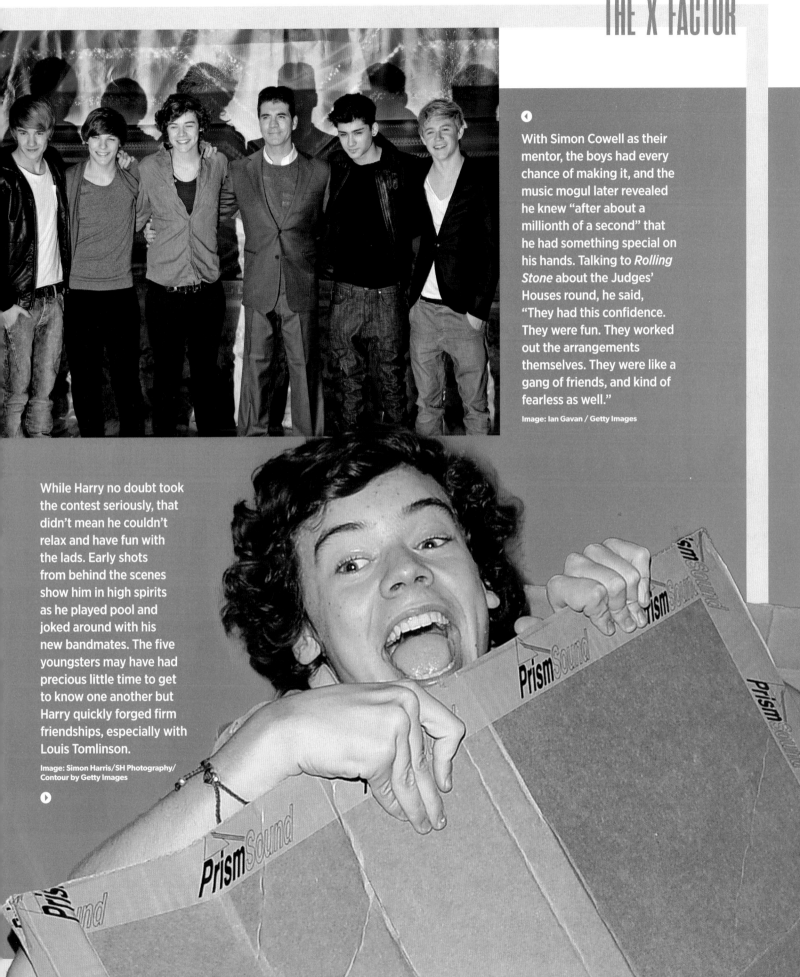

With Simon Cowell as their mentor, the boys had every chance of making it, and the music mogul later revealed he knew "after about a millionth of a second" that he had something special on his hands. Talking to *Rolling Stone* about the Judges' Houses round, he said, "They had this confidence. They were fun. They worked out the arrangements themselves. They were like a gang of friends, and kind of fearless as well."

Image: Ian Gavan / Getty Images

While Harry no doubt took the contest seriously, that didn't mean he couldn't relax and have fun with the lads. Early shots from behind the scenes show him in high spirits as he played pool and joked around with his new bandmates. The five youngsters may have had precious little time to get to know one another but Harry quickly forged firm friendships, especially with Louis Tomlinson.

Image: Simon Harris/SH Photography/ Contour by Getty Images

Right from the early days on the show, Harry emerged as a born leader. Simon Cowell later called him "memorable and a natural frontman", saying, "I thought, 'This kid's got everything: he's really confident, he's got unbelievable charisma, and he's a good singer'... He was exactly what you're looking for when you make one of these shows."

Image: Ken McKay / Talkback Thames /Shutterstock

Did you know?

Harry may have sold over 15 million albums, but reports suggest he wasn't always confident in his singing ability. His childhood friend Nick Clough says that when Harry joined school mates to form their band, White Eskimo, he worried his vocals wouldn't be up to scratch. "When he first joined the band Harry didn't think he could sing and was worried people would laugh," said Nick. He added, "Being in the band really helped his confidence because people used to say he was a really good singer."

◄ With their fanbase rapidly growing, Harry and the other *X Factor* hopefuls stepped out on the showbiz circuit. By now they had been given slick hairstyles, and clothes to match. At the London premiere of *The Chronicles Of Narnia: The Voyage Of The Dawn* they walked the red carpet and rubbed shoulders with actors including Liam Neeson, Will Poulter and Simon Pegg. And they were in excellent company – the late Queen was also in attendance.

Gareth Cattermole / Getty Images

◄ As the live shows gathered pace, Harry and the band got used to life in the limelight. Whether they were walking the streets of London or nipping out to the supermarket, they were mobbed by fans and the paparazzi, eager to snap shots of the rising stars. Life had certainly taken an unexpected turn for Harry, who just months earlier had been just another teenager, splitting his time between school and a £6 an hour Saturday job.

Image: Neil Mockford / FilmMagic /Getty

Harry is famed for his fashion credentials, and even during his time on *The X Factor* he showed glimpses of the flamboyant sense of style we now know so well. From chunky knits to skinny scarves and his infamous white onesie, he was clearly having fun with fashion. He also enjoyed posing for his first photoshoots too, looking remarkably at ease in front of the camera for a tender 16 year old.

Image: Simon Harris/SH Photography/Contour by Getty Images

Nearly 18 million people tuned in to watch the final of *The X Factor* on 12 December 2010. While Harry and the rest of One Direction were thrilled to be joined by Robbie Williams to sing 'She's the One', it wasn't enough for them to win. But ultimately, the result didn't matter. Within hours, Simon had signed them to his record label, and they were firmly on the road to global stardom.

Image: Ken McKay / Talkback Thames / Shutterstock

Fun Fact

HE MAY HAVE LOOKED COOL AND CHARISMATIC WHENEVER HE TOOK TO THE STAGE DURING *THE X FACTOR*, BUT REPORTS SUGGEST THAT HARRY SOMETIMES SUFFERED SEVERE BOUTS OF STAGE FRIGHT. IT'S EVEN SAID THAT HIS NERVES WERE SO BAD, THEY MADE HIM VOMIT – AND THAT SIMON COWELL CONSIDERED ASKING HIS CELEBRITY PAL, HYPNOTIST PAUL MCKENNA, TO HELP. LATER, BANDMATE LIAM SPOKE ABOUT IT, SAYING, "HARRY DOES GET QUITE SCARED... HE WENT THROUGH A PERIOD OF THROWING UP BEFORE HE WENT ON STAGE. I THINK HE'S OVER IT NOW THOUGH."

Image: Danny Martindale / FilmMagic / Getty Images

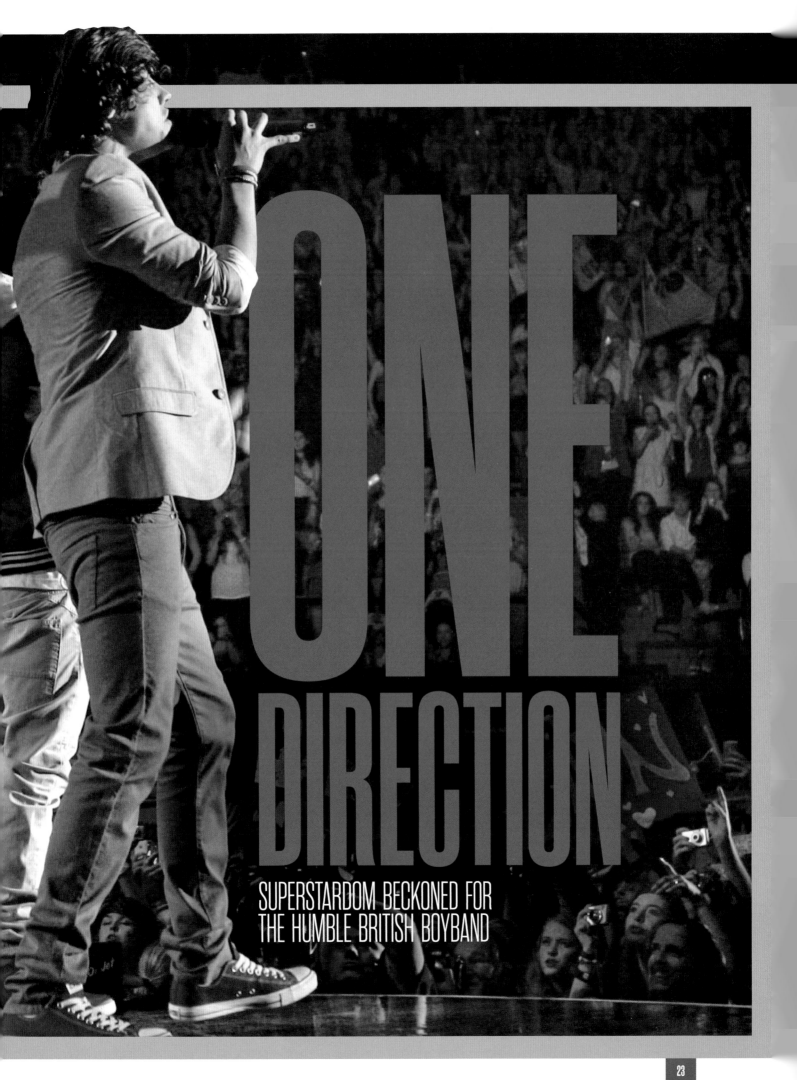

ONE DIRECTION

SUPERSTARDOM BECKONED FOR
THE HUMBLE BRITISH BOYBAND

They may not have won the coveted *X Factor* crown, but it wouldn't be long before One Direction hit the big time. After spending Christmas at home with friends and family, Simon Cowell flew them out to America. There they stayed in Los Angeles, where the music mogul introduced them to the major players in the industry.

Image: Dave Hogan / Getty Images

The much-anticipated X Factor Tour followed, giving Harry and the band a chance to get used to performing in packed-out stadiums across the UK. The band took to the stage alongside the likes of Matt Cardle, Rebecca Ferguson and Cher Lloyd, before they took a step back from live shows in order to begin working in earnest on their first album.

Mark Cuthbert / Getty Images

From private flights in luxury helicopters to a skiing holiday, life in the limelight was very different to what any of the boys were used to. Harry was mobbed by hysterical fans wherever he went, desperate for an autograph or selfie with the star. Offers flooded in for appearances and endorsements too.

Image: Dave Hogan / Getty Images

He might have been
working hard, but Harry
was having the time of his
life. He and the band had
formed firm friendships,
and they soon moved
into a luxury apartment
complex in North London.
Harry and Louis shared a
£5,000 a month bachelor
pad in the development,
which even had its own
gym and – importantly for
the budding megastars –
round the clock security.

Image: Fred Duval / FilmMagic / Getty images

In September 2011, One Direction launched
their much-anticipated first single, 'What
Makes You Beautiful', with a signing at
HMV Oxford Street. The lads were in high
spirits, and their exuberance was no doubt
boosted further when it took the number
one spot. The happy-go-lucky track
topped the charts for four consecutive
weeks, also making the top ten in Australia,
Canada, Japan and the USA, and is today
still one of their most iconic songs.

Image: Fred Duval / FilmMagic / Getty images

Fun Fact

HARRY AND THE BOYS DAZZLED
ON THEIR FIRST EVER LIVE
TOUR, WINNING DEAFENING
SHRIEKS OF APPROVAL FROM
THE EXCITED CROWDS. BUT
ONE THING MARKED THEM
APART FROM MANY OTHER
BOYBANDS – THEY DIDN'T
DO CHOREOGRAPHED DANCE
ROUTINES. "WE JUST KIND
OF CAME OUT AND SAID, 'WE
CAN'T DANCE. WE'RE A BIT
LAZY. WE'RE JUST NORMAL
LADS," LIAM, SAID IN AN
INTERVIEW WITH *GLAMOUR*.
HARRY ADDED, "THE
THING IS, WHEN YOU'RE
PLAYING A PART,
EVENTUALLY IT GOES
WRONG... EVENTUALLY
SOMEONE'S GOING TO SEE
THAT THAT'S NOT
WHO YOU ARE. SO
IT'S BEST TO BE
YOURSELF FROM
THE GET-GO."

Image: Michael Buckner /Getty images

ONE DIRECTION

In February 2012, Harry appeared at the BRIT Awards in a grey suit and bowtie – a big change from the T-shirts and hoodies he'd been wearing just a few months before. The boys were overjoyed when One Direction won the coveted Best British Single gong, for 'What Makes You Beautiful', beating off competition from Ed Sheeran and Adele. It would be the first of seven BRITs for the band, who scored almost 200 awards.

Image: Gareth Cattermole / Getty Images

IN FEBRUARY 2012, HARRY APPEARED AT THE BRIT AWARDS, LOOKING SHARP IN A GREY SUIT AND BOWTIE

Did you know?

HARRY AND THE BOYS MADE THREE APPEARANCES ON HIT US SHOW *SATURDAY NIGHT LIVE*, AND HE'S SINCE STARRED TWICE ON THE SHOW IN HIS OWN RIGHT. ONE DIRECTION'S DEBUT WAS AN INSTANT HIT – THEY SANG 'WHAT MAKES YOU BEAUTIFUL' AND 'ONE THING' FROM THEIR FIRST ALBUM, *UP ALL NIGHT*. THEY THEN PERFORMED WHAT WOULD PROVE TO BE THE FIRST OF MANY SKETCHES ON THE SHOW, THIS TIME ALONGSIDE THEN-HOST, *MODERN FAMILY*'S SOFIA VERGARA.

Image: Dana Edelson / NBCU Photo Bank / NBCUniversal via Getty Images

After America it was on to Australia, New Zealand and then back to New York for the *Men In Black* movie premiere. Eventually, Harry touched down back on UK soil, where he was pictured looking at houses in London. He was also snapped shopping at designer Dolce & Gabbana and attending a Burberry fashion show, showing a hint of the love of high fashion that was to come.

Image: Neil Mockford / Film Magic / Getty

◀ March 2012 saw Harry jetting back to America, where the band appeared at the Nickelodeon Kids' Choice Awards, singing 'What Makes You Beautiful'. They may have been relatively new on the pop scene, but the crowd – which included Taylor Swift and even Michelle Obama – went wild, singing and clapping along.

Image: Jeff Kravitz / FilmMagic / Getty images

▲ Harry's fresh-faced good looks made him a pin-up for millions of fans across the globe. Here, he's pictured greeting a crowd of adoring girls at the MTV Video Music Awards in Los Angeles, where they won their first MTV award. One fan reportedly adored the singer so much, she made a shrine out of a plastic water bottle that he threw into the crowd at a concert.

Image: Kevin Mazur / WireImage / Getty images

In late 2012, Harry Styles fans went into meltdown when a cute picture emerged of the handsome teen walking through Central Park in New York with Taylor Swift. It soon emerged that the pair were dating and although their romance only lasted a few months, the relationship inspired some of their future music.

Image: David Krieger / Bauer-Griffin / GC Images

2013 was a huge year for Harry and the band. They won numerous awards – including two more BRIT awards – and rocked out at over 130 shows on their Take Me Home Tour, performing for millions of fans. The gruelling tour lasted for over six months, taking them to America, Australia, Japan, Mexico and Europe.

Image: Brian Rasic / Getty Images

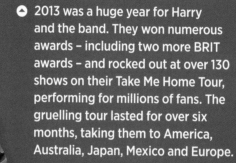

IN LATE 2012, FANS WENT INTO MELTDOWN WHEN A PICTURE EMERGED OF HARRY IN NEW YORK WITH TAYLOR SWIFT

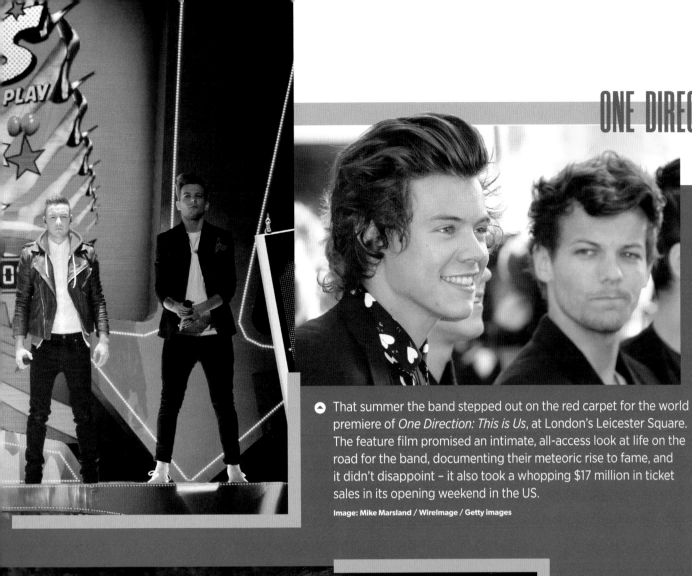

⬤ That summer the band stepped out on the red carpet for the world premiere of *One Direction: This is Us*, at London's Leicester Square. The feature film promised an intimate, all-access look at life on the road for the band, documenting their meteoric rise to fame, and it didn't disappoint – it also took a whopping $17 million in ticket sales in its opening weekend in the US.

Image: Mike Marsland / WireImage / Getty images

◀ Meanwhile, Harry's emerging sense of style clearly wasn't going unnoticed – he was spotted on the front row at fashion shows and showed off his credentials at a private dinner hosted by British designer, Sir Paul Smith. There he rubbed shoulders with Radio DJ Nick Grimshaw, rapper Tinie Tempah and TV host James Corden.

Image: Dave M. Benett / Getty Images

Harry and the band may have had to grow up fast, but every so often their mischievous antics proved they were still kids at heart. When they appeared for an interview on a New York radio show, the boys were presented with a giant cake, decorated with the Union Jack flag. But instead of tucking in, they cheerfully dunked Harry's face into it. He later tweeted: "I just got caked in the face... and a cake made of ice cream is harder than regular cake. Hard cake in the face."

Image: Paul Zimmerman / WireImage

In November 2013, Cindy Crawford joined Harry and the band for part of 1D Day, a seven-hour livestream event involving celebrity appearances and songs from their album, *Midnight Memories*. The legendary supermodel even watched Liam and Harry strike their best poses on a catwalk, before joining them herself.

Image: Jeff Kravitz / FilmMagic / Getty

Ever popular thanks to his kind, easy-going nature, Harry often rubbed shoulders with other A-listers. Here he is at the Burberry Prorsum Womenswear Spring / Summer 2014 show, alongside singer Paloma Faith, actress Sienna Miller and model Suki Waterhouse. He reportedly dated supermodel Kendall Jenner on and off between 2013 and 2016 too.

Image: David M. Benett / Getty Images for Burberry

Fun Fact

HARRY AND THE BOYS EVEN HAD THEIR OWN WAXWORKS MADE AT MADAME TUSSAUDS. HERE IS HARRY, BEING MEASURED UP FOR HIS. "WE'RE JUST KIND OF A BIT OVERWHELMED," HE ADMITTED AT THE TIME. "WE'VE BEEN TO MADAME TUSSAUDS AND SEEN THE KIND OF PEOPLE WHO ARE IN THERE. IT'S CRAZY TO THINK THAT WE WILL BE UP THERE WITH THEM." ONE DIRECTION'S MODELS WERE AMONG THE BIGGEST DRAWS AT THE LEGENDARY ATTRACTION, UNTIL THEY WERE RETIRED TO THE BAKER STREET ARCHIVE IN EARLY 2022. THE NEWS SPARKED A FRENZY FROM FANS, WHO SENT MESSAGES ASKING TO TAKE OWNERSHIP OF THE FIGURES – WITH SOME BEGGING FOR HARRY'S HEAD.

Image: Madame Tussauds / Getty Images

In November 2014, pop royalty met genuine royalty when Harry was introduced to the Princess of Wales – then the Duchess of Cambridge – at The Royal Variety Performance. Catherine, who was pregnant with Princess Charlotte, looked delighted to meet the handsome heart-throb. "I said congratulations on the bump," Harry said afterwards. "[Though] she didn't look bumpy."

Image: Yui Mok - WPA Pool / Getty Images

2014 also saw One Direction win yet another BRIT Award, this time for their global success. But Harry very nearly missed his moment of triumph, because he was in the loo when Liam, Louis, Niall and Zayn came up to receive their accolade. Dashing onto the stage at the 11th hour, he told the crowd, "I'm really sorry I was having a wee, the toilets are ages away!"

Image: Brian Rasic / Getty Images

Did you know?

Harry's body is covered in works of art. The singer has over 60 tattoos, many on a nautical theme. As well as an anchor, pirate ship and mermaid, he counts two swallows, a giant rose and a large butterfly among his designs. Harry got his first tattoo – a star on his bicep – to celebrate his 18th birthday and once even let Ed Sheeran ink a padlock on his wrist. While he loves his body art, it can take time to conceal it when he does a film shoot or music video. "It's the only time I regret getting tattooed," he said.

Image: Neil Mockford / GC Images / Getty images

Harry and the band closed out 2014 with another comedy skit on *Saturday Night Live*, also performing their hit, 'Night Changes'. They dressed up in tracksuits and pretended to be a dance troupe, alongside actress Amy Adams, proving that their sense of humour remained intact, despite the fact they were looking increasingly exhausted by their gruelling schedules.

Image: Dana Edelson / NBCU Photo Bank / NBCUniversal via Getty Images via Getty Images

In March 2015, news broke that Zayn had left One Direction's On The Road Again Tour, due to stress. He then dropped the bombshell that he was quitting the band, and later outraged fans by saying he wanted to make music that was "cool". Harry was diplomatic when asked about his bandmate's decision, saying, "We were sad, obviously, that someone had left, but also sad that he was not enjoying it so much that he had to leave."

Image: Kevin Winter /Getty Images for iHeartMedia

The band finished their tour without Zayn, before returning to LA. There, a fresh-faced Harry revealed he was following a juice cleanse, saying that he'd "felt a little gross" after flying so much. The star certainly takes care to look after his mental and physical wellbeing, refusing to take drugs during his days with the band. He has also turned to yoga and Pilates to help his back, and is a fan of meditation too.

Image: Olivia Salazar / WireImage / Getty

Did you know?

WORLD TOURS MAY BE PACKED WITH EXCITEMENT AND ADRENALIN, BUT THEY ALSO INVOLVE CONSTANT TRAVEL, HARD GRAFT AND SPENDING TIME AWAY FROM FAMILY AND FRIENDS. BOTH SIMON COWELL AND LIAM PAYNE HAVE ADMITTED THAT ONE DIRECTION WERE OVERWORKED, WITH SIMON SAYING, "EVEN THOUGH THEY WERE YOUNG, THAT WAS A GRUELLING SCHEDULE... AFTER A WHILE I COULD SEE THEY WERE EXHAUSTED." HARRY'S FRIEND NICK GRIMSHAW HAS SPOKEN OUT TOO, SAYING, "PEOPLE THINK BEING A POP STAR IS GLAMOROUS BUT IT'S EXHAUSTING AND DISORIENTING AT THEIR LEVEL," HE SAID. "THEY DON'T SEE THE WORLD, THEY JUST DO PRESS IN DIFFERENT CITIES."

Image: Jason Merritt /Getty Images for iHeartMedia

Despite being a member down, Harry and the band continued doing what they loved – giving stellar performances in front of millions of fans. But making five albums and doing four world tours was no doubt taking its toll, and rumours began to swirl that it wouldn't be long before they took a break.

Image: Steve Jennings / WireImage / Getty images

RUMOURS BEGAN TO SWIRL THAT IT WOULDN'T BE LONG BEFORE THE BAND TOOK A BREAK

In August 2015, Harry, Louis, Liam and Niall confirmed the news that fans dreaded – One Direction would indeed take a hiatus the following year. Harry later told *Rolling Stone*, "If you're shortsighted, you can think, 'Let's just keep touring,' but we all thought too much of the group than to let that happen. You realise you're exhausted and you don't want to drain people's belief in you."

Image: Kevin Mazur /AMA2015 / WireImage

Fittingly, One Direction made their final performance on *The X Factor* stage – the very show that had launched their careers five years before. After performing and watching video messages from the likes of Robbie Williams, David Beckham and Little Mix, Harry shared an emotional hug with his bandmates. "I love the band, and would never rule out anything in the future," he later said. "The band changed my life, gave me everything."

Image: Cooper Neill / Getty Images for iHeartMedia

ING SOLO

HARRY FOUND
HIS OWN VOICE
— AND QUICKLY
BECAME A
GLOBAL ICON

● Harry kicked off 2016 by parting ways with his management of five years and joining forces with top US agent, Jeffrey Azoff. He stayed out of the limelight at first and when fans finally caught a glimpse of the singer, he was barely recognisable. His trademark long locks had vanished, along with his boyband image.

Image: FRANCOIS LO PRESTI /AFP via Getty Images

But Harry hadn't left the music world behind – far from it. In June 2016, he signed a solo contract with Columbia Records, the same label behind One Direction. In May 2017, he then released his first solo single, 'Sign Of The Times', followed by his debut solo album, called *Harry Styles.*

Image: James Devaney / GC Images / Getty
Patricia Schlein/Star Max / GC Images

HIS TRADEMARK LONG LOCKS HAD VANISHED, ALONG WITH HIS BOYBAND IMAGE

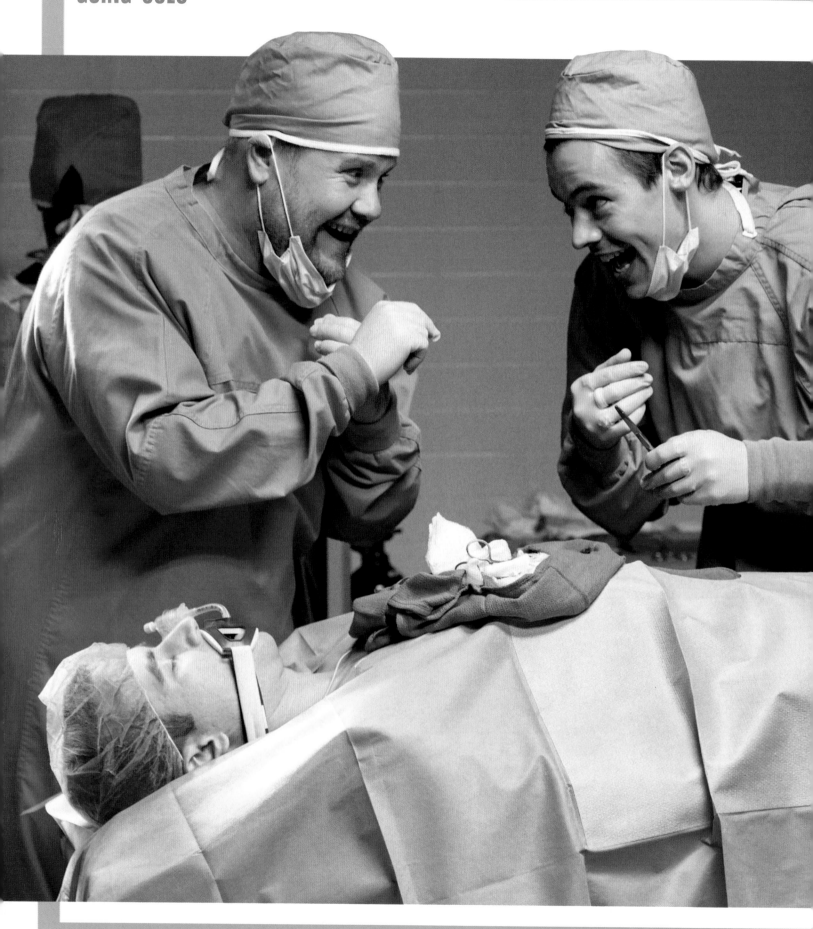

Harry proved his comedy credentials when he joined pal James Corden for a week-long residency on *The Late Late Show*. The week included an impressive line-up of musical comedy skits, including one where Harry and James kept bursting into upbeat songs at inappropriate times. One side-splitting segment showed them breaking into a rendition of 'It's Not Unusual' while pretending to be surgeons in the operating theatre, and 'Mambo No. 5' while acting as pallbearers at a mock funeral.

Image: Terence Patrick / CBS via Getty Images

● The week culminated with a memorable session of Carpool Karaoke, in which they rocked out to 'Sign Of The Times', as well as Harry's other songs, 'Sweet Creature' and 'Kiwi'. Harry also admitted that he sometimes cried while performing his hit single.

Image: Terence Patrick /CBS via Getty Images

Fun Fact

HARRY CUT OFF HIS FAMOUS BRUNETTE LOCKS FOR CHARITY, DOING WONDERS FOR THE LITTLE PRINCESS TRUST. SINCE 2006 THE ORGANISATION HAS HELPED PROVIDE OVER 12,000 WIGS MADE FROM REAL HAIR FOR CHILDREN SUFFERING FROM HAIR LOSS, DUE TO CANCER TREATMENT OR OTHER CONDITIONS. THE POPSTAR'S KIND-HEARTED GESTURE CAUSED THE CHARITY'S FACEBOOK AND TWITTER FOLLOWERS TO DRAMATICALLY INCREASE, AND PEOPLE ACROSS THE GLOBE PLEDGED DONATIONS TOO. DELIGHTED CO-FOUNDER WENDY TARPLEE-MORRIS SAID, "A LITTLE WHILE BACK HE [HARRY] HAD EXPRESSED AN INTEREST IN SUPPORTING US... AND THEN ALL OF A SUDDEN HE DID IT."

Image: Jon Kopaloff/FilmMagic / Getty images

Did you know?

THE EXPRESSION 'TREAT PEOPLE WITH KINDNESS' BECAME SOMETHING OF A MOTTO FOR HARRY DURING HIS 2018 TOUR. IT BEGAN AS A MESSAGE ON HIS GUITAR STRAP, BUT HE SOON STARTED MAKING T-SHIRTS FEATURING THE SLOGAN AND IT LATER INSPIRED A HIT SONG, WITH AN UPLIFTING VIDEO STARRING HIM AND *FLEABAG* STAR PHOEBE WALLER-BRIDGE. HERE HE IS CELEBRATING THE BRIT AWARDS WITH PALOMA FAITH, WEARING THE MANTRA ON A PIN BADGE. "SMALL CHANGES END UP MAKING A BIG DIFFERENCE," HE SAID. "IT'S ABOUT BEING A LOT NICER TO EACH OTHER RATHER THAN, 'DON'T DO THIS, OR DON'T DO THAT, NOT THIS, YES THAT.' IT'S JUST SAYING, 'TREAT PEOPLE WITH KINDNESS.'"

Images: Richard Young / Shutterstock

'Sign Of The Times' was an instant hit with both fans and music critics alike. It shot straight to number one, knocking Ed Sheeran off the top spot, and was certified platinum in both the US and UK. Harry Styles also peaked at number one in more than 20 countries, and when the singer embarked on his first solo tour, he proved he had powerful command of the stage.

Image: James D. Morgan /WireImage / Getty images

Harry's debut solo tour was such a storming success that extra dates were quickly added, taking the run up to 89 shows. Tickets for the first leg sold out in an incredible 29 seconds, with the singer fast earning a name for his dazzling performances. He was applauded for his attitude to inclusivity and diversity too, waving Black Lives Matter flags and raising $1.2 million in charity donations.

Image: Rich Fury / Getty Images for iHeartMedia
Rich Fury / Getty Images Entertainment
Getty Images North America

HARRY'S DEBUT SOLO TOUR WAS SUCH A STORMING SUCCESS THAT EXTRA DATES WERE QUICKLY ADDED

In November 2019, Harry hosted and was the musical guest for *Saturday Night Live*. Once again, he showed off his sparkling comedic skills, playing a gangster, Icelandic dad-to-be and an airline pilot, who made hilarious Scooby Doo and Shaggy impressions, unaware that the bemused passengers can hear him over the intercom.

Image: Will Heath / NBC / NBCU Photo Bank via Getty Images

Did you know?

Harry is famous for his flamboyant tour costumes, and many of them are custom-made pieces, designed by Gucci's creative director Alessandro Michele. Alessandro is widely credited for the singer's style transformation. Harry is a long-time fan of the Italian fashion house, frequently rocking everything from vibrant floral suits to harlequin jackets and flared trousers. And in 2018, it was revealed he would become the face of the new Gucci tailoring campaign.

Image: Steve Jennings/Getty Images for Sony Music

▶ Harry also played two songs from his upcoming album *Fine Line* on the show, debuting 'Watermelon Sugar'. He belted out the hit single wearing a vibrant red suit and heels, adding an extra pop of colour with his pink and blue nails.

Image: Will Heath / NBC / NBCU Photo Bank via Getty Images

◀ *Fine Line,* Harry's second album, broke records on its December release, making the singing sensation the first UK male artist to top the charts with his first two albums. The LA-based star was all set for a worldwide tour in 2020, but the COVID-19 pandemic put paid to his plans and it was postponed until the following year.

Image: Terence Patrick / CBS via Getty Images

In 2019, Harry was thrilled to co-chair the Met Gala, one of the biggest events on the fashion calendar. Smiling as he stepped out on the red carpet, the singer soon got stuck into the party spirit for the night. Here he is alongside Gucci's Alessandro Michele, wearing a semi sheer black lace jumpsuit which showed off his many tattoos. He teamed it with patent high heels, and a pearl drop earring.

Image: Theo Wargo / WireImage /Getty

IN 2019, HARRY CO-CHAIRED THE MET GALA, ONE OF THE BIGGEST EVENTS IN FASHION

Fun Fact

KIND-HEARTED HARRY HAS RAISED MILLIONS FOR CHARITY OVER THE YEARS. AS WELL AS GIVING HIS HAIR TO THE LITTLE PRINCESS TRUST AND RAISING FUNDS THROUGH HIS MERCHANDISING, HE HAS ALSO DONATED SIGNED GUITARS TO CHARITY AUCTIONS. THIS CHERRY RED GIBSON GUITAR SOLD FOR AN INCREDIBLE $28,125 IN 2020, OVER NINE TIMES ITS ESTIMATE OF $3,000. THE PROCEEDS PROVIDED MUCH-NEEDED FUNDS FOR MUSICARES, A CHARITABLE FOUNDATION SUPPORTING PEOPLE IN THE MUSIC INDUSTRY, WHICH WAS SO BADLY AFFECTED BY THE CANCELLATION OF LIVE SHOWS DURING THE PANDEMIC. HARRY SIGNED THE GUITAR IN SILVER PEN, WRITING HIS MANTRA, 'TREAT PEOPLE WITH KINDNESS'.

GOING SOLO

▶ It may have been a challenging year, but Harry still scooped multiple awards in 2020. He won Best International Artist at the 2020 ARIAs, the Billboard Chart Achievement Award and his first Global Award, for 'Lights Up', which he received over video link. *Variety* also named him Hitmaker of the Year for his critically acclaimed second album, *Fine Line*.

Image: Jeff Kravitz / FilmMagic for Sony Music

▼

Harry sang 'Falling' at the 2020 BRIT Awards, and it was an emotionally charged performance. Earlier that evening he had arrived on the red carpet wearing a black ribbon on his jacket. The gesture was thought to be in tribute to his close friend, TV presenter Caroline Flack, who had died just days before.

Image: Samir Hussein / WireImage / Getty images

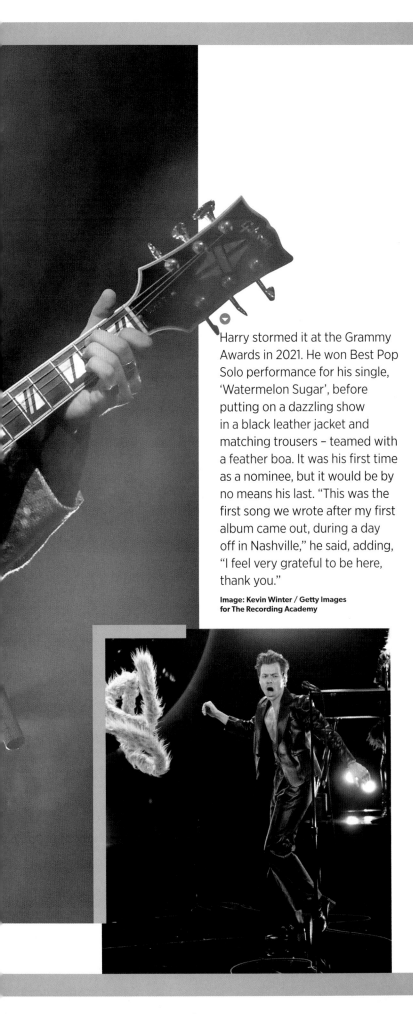

Harry stormed it at the Grammy Awards in 2021. He won Best Pop Solo performance for his single, 'Watermelon Sugar', before putting on a dazzling show in a black leather jacket and matching trousers – teamed with a feather boa. It was his first time as a nominee, but it would be by no means his last. "This was the first song we wrote after my first album came out, during a day off in Nashville," he said, adding, "I feel very grateful to be here, thank you."

Image: Kevin Winter / Getty Images for The Recording Academy

Did you know?

HARRY TURNED TO WRITING AND PLAYING MUSIC DURING LOCKDOWN. WITH HIS PLANNED TOUR POSTPONED, THE SINGER FOUND HIMSELF TAKING A BREAK FROM HIS HECTIC WORK SCHEDULE FOR THE FIRST TIME SINCE *THE X FACTOR*. TRYING TO "STAY POSITIVE AND STAY PRODUCTIVE", HE SPENT HIS DAYS MEDITATING, WORKING OUT AND PLAYING THE PIANO AND GUITAR. "I'VE BEEN WRITING SO MUCH," HE SAID. "I SHOULD BE PLAYING THE PIANO MORE… I SHOULD BE PLAYING THE GUITAR MORE. I SHOULD BE WRITING POEMS AND LYRICS MORE. SO I'VE BEEN DOING A LOT OF THAT."

Images: Kevin Winter / Getty Images for The Recording Academy

Harry's slick and sexy Grammy look was a marked departure from his favoured floral suits. It showed off the big butterfly tattoo on his stomach, as well as the two swallows he had tattooed on his chest when he was just 18. "I got two swallows on my chest," Harry said at the time. "I like that kind of style of tattoos, like the old sailor kind of tattoos. They symbolise travelling, and we travel a lot!" He also admitted the inking was painful, saying, "Anyone who says tattoos don't hurt is a liar!"

Image: Kevin Winter / Getty Images for The Recording Academy

Did you know?

Harry has spoken openly about mental health, revealing that he was at first resistant to trying therapy. "I think for a long time I was like, 'I don't need that'," he said. "You know, it's very like British way of looking at it." However, he was persuaded to try it after One Direction, and credits it with changing his perspective. "I think that accepting living, being happy, hurting in the extremes, that is the most alive you can be," he said. "Losing it crying, losing it laughing – there's no way, I don't think, to feel more alive than that."

Image: Dia Dipasupil / Getty Images Entertainment

2021 saw Harry winning his second BRIT Award, this time for 'Watermelon Sugar'. He strode onto the stage in a retro Gucci Aria suit, looking emotional at the accolade. "I continue to be baffled by moments like this," he said, thanking his fans and friends. "They make me more and more incredibly grateful to get to do this job every day."

Image: JMEnternational / JMEnternational for BRIT Awards / Getty Images

In April 2022, Harry wowed the crowd at Coachella, when he donned a glitzy sequin catsuit for his high-octane headline act. The strutting showman sang hits, including 'Adore You', 'As It Was' and 'Watermelon Sugar' at the California festival, winning plaudits for his dazzling performance.

Image: Kevin Mazur / Getty Images for ABA

For the second week of the festival, Harry traded his sparkling catsuit for shimmering, shocking pink trousers and a voluminous feathered coat. Fans were thrilled when he introduced Lizzo as a surprise guest, with the pair singing Gloria Gaynor's 'I Will Survive'. Humble as ever, Harry thanked his fans, saying, "Coachella, each and every single one of you thank you so so much." He added, "life is all about moments, and this is one I will not forget."

Image: Kevin Mazur / Getty Images

> 2022 also saw the release of the superstar's third solo album, *Harry's House*, which would later scoop him Album of the Year at MTV's VMAs. In an electrifying show at BBC Radio 1's Big Weekend in Coventry, he performed a series of his newest tracks, including 'Daylight', 'Music For A Sushi Restaurant' and 'As It Was'. His costume didn't disappoint either – this time he rocked a black and purple sequinned jumpsuit.

Did you know?

ONE OF HARRY'S BIGGEST INSPIRATIONS IS CANADIAN COUNTRY STAR SHANIA TWAIN. "I'M LIKE A MASSIVE SHANIA TWAIN FAN... SHE'S AMAZING," HE TOLD JOOLS HOLLAND BACK IN 2019. FAST FORWARD THREE YEARS AND THE SINGER JOINED HIM ON STAGE AT COACHELLA FOR A SURPRISE PERFORMANCE OF TWO OF HER HITS, 'MAN! I FEEL LIKE A WOMAN' AND 'YOU'RE STILL THE ONE'. CHATTING TO THE ROARING CROWD, HARRY REVEALED, "I HAVE TO TELL YOU, IN THE CAR, WITH MY MOTHER AS A CHILD, THIS LADY TAUGHT ME TO SING." HE ADDED, "SHE ALSO TAUGHT ME THAT MEN ARE TRASH."

IN AN ELECTRIFYING SHOW AT BBC RADIO 1'S BIG WEEKEND, HE PERFORMED A SERIES OF HIS NEWEST TRACKS

Just when you thought Harry couldn't get any bigger, he added more dates to his sell-out show, Love On Tour. The tour was due to end in December 2022 but has now been extended until July 2023, when it will take him to Asia, Europe and back to the UK, for nine much-anticipated nights.

Image: Gilbert Carrasquillo / GC Images

NEW

HORIZONS

NOT CONTENT WITH BECOMING A MUSICAL
LEGEND, HARRY SHONE ON THE SILVER SCREEN

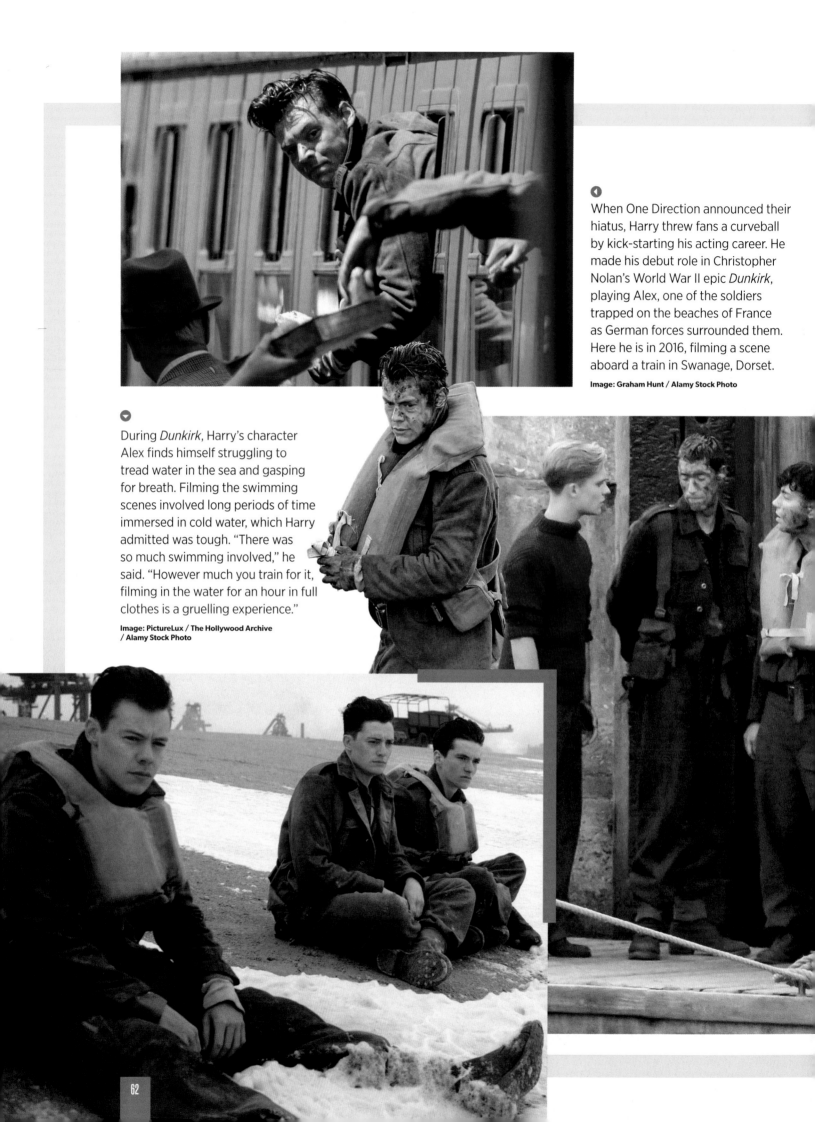

When One Direction announced their hiatus, Harry threw fans a curveball by kick-starting his acting career. He made his debut role in Christopher Nolan's World War II epic *Dunkirk*, playing Alex, one of the soldiers trapped on the beaches of France as German forces surrounded them. Here he is in 2016, filming a scene aboard a train in Swanage, Dorset.

Image: Graham Hunt / Alamy Stock Photo

During *Dunkirk*, Harry's character Alex finds himself struggling to tread water in the sea and gasping for breath. Filming the swimming scenes involved long periods of time immersed in cold water, which Harry admitted was tough. "There was so much swimming involved," he said. "However much you train for it, filming in the water for an hour in full clothes is a gruelling experience."

Image: PictureLux / The Hollywood Archive / Alamy Stock Photo

Despite his fame, Harry still said he found it "overwhelming" walking on set for the first time. But he needn't have worried – he earned rave reviews for his star turn. He even admitted to pal Nick Grimshaw that he found the world premiere emotional. "There were a couple of emotional bits but I didn't know if I was allowed to cry at a film I'm in," he modestly revealed on Radio 1.

Image: Graham Hunt / Alamy Stock Photo

Did you know?

HARRY STARS ALONGSIDE KENNETH BRANAGH AND TOM HARDY IN *DUNKIRK*, BUT WHEN HE AUDITIONED FOR THE ROLE, DIRECTOR CHRISTOPHER NOLAN DIDN'T REALISE HE WAS A GLOBAL SUPERSTAR TOO. "I DON'T THINK I WAS THAT AWARE REALLY OF HOW FAMOUS HARRY WAS," HE TOLD *THE HOLLYWOOD REPORTER*. "THE TRUTH IS, I CAST HARRY BECAUSE HE FIT THE PART WONDERFULLY." NOLAN, WHO CALLED HARRY "A NATURAL," HAS ALSO SAID HE CAST HIM BECAUSE HE HAS "THE KIND OF FACE THAT MAKES YOU BELIEVE HE COULD HAVE BEEN ALIVE IN THAT PERIOD". "HARRY'S CHARACTER'S VERY UNGLAMOROUS," HE SAID. "IT'S NOT A SHOWBOATING ROLE. AND HARRY SHIED AWAY FROM BEING A 'STAR'. HE'S A HUMBLE GUY WHO DIDN'T WANT ATTENTION."

Images: Kevin Mazur /Getty Images

Harry isn't just an accomplished actor, he's a great TV presenter too. In December 2019, he showcased his many talents when he stood in for James Corden to guest-host *The Late Late Show*. In addition to welcoming ex-girlfriend Kendall Jenner and *Girlfriends* actress Tracee Ellis Ross onto the couch, he filmed a mini version of Carpool Karaoke, delivered the show's opening monologue and performed his hit, 'Adore You'.

Image: Terence Patrick / CBS via Getty Images

Harry's co-hosting stint included challenging Kendall to a hilarious game of Spill Your Guts, the show's legendary truth-telling skit. While Kendall chose to sip a salmon smoothie over divulging who the "most unlikeable" supermodel is, Harry refused to rank his former bandmates' solo careers. Instead, he ate a giant water scorpion.

Image: Terence Patrick / CBS via Getty Images

Harry once again showed off his brilliant comic timing with a double whammy, acting as both host and musical guest on hit US show, *Saturday Night Live*. Sitting down at a piano for his opening monologue, he joked about life after One Direction, saying, "I don't know if you've heard or not but... I'm not in a boyband anymore. I'm in a man band now."

Image: Will Heath / NBC / NBCU Photo Bank via Getty Images

IN DECEMBER 2019, HARRY SHOWCASED HIS MANY TALENTS WHEN HE STOOD IN FOR JAMES CORDEN TO GUEST-HOST *THE LATE LATE SHOW*

NEW HORIZONS

Harry became friends with triple Grammy Award winner Lizzo in 2019, and their friendship has spawned some dazzling duets. The pair first joined forces onstage in 2020, when they performed her hit 'Juice' during Super Bowl week. The playful performance even saw Lizzo pretend to spank Harry, before the pair closed out the show with a confetti shower.

Image: Kevin Mazur / Getty Images for Pandora

Later on the show, he thrilled fans with a sparkling skit as a funeral DJ, alongside comedian Chris Redd. The hilarious scene culminated with Harry and Chris ripping off their trousers to reveal tight white pants emblazoned with the words RIP BETTY, before shaking their hips to the hit 'Everybody Dance Now'.

Image: John Shearer / Getty Images for Sandbox Entertainment

Harry hasn't just collaborated with stars on TV, he has also has delighted fans with his musical duets. In 2018, he and American country singer Kacey Musgraves performed an electrifying cover of Shania Twain's 'You're Still the One'. They reunited on stage the following year, when Kacey brought Harry onstage at her concert in Nashville, to duet her hit, 'Space Cowboy'.

Image: Will Heath / NBC / NBCU Photo Bank via Getty Images

⊙ Harry is a huge Fleetwood Mac fan, and the band's hit 'Dreams' was the first song he knew all the words to. "I used to sing it in the car with my mum," he revealed. Since he became pals with singer Stevie Nicks, the pair have delighted fans with their co-performances, including several duets of the Fleetwood Mac ballad, 'Landslide'. Stevie has even dedicated the hit to Harry at her concerts, and during lockdown she revealed she was listening to his album *Fine Line*, which was inspiring her to "write some new songs and poetry."

Image: Jeff Kravitz / FilmMagic / Getty Images

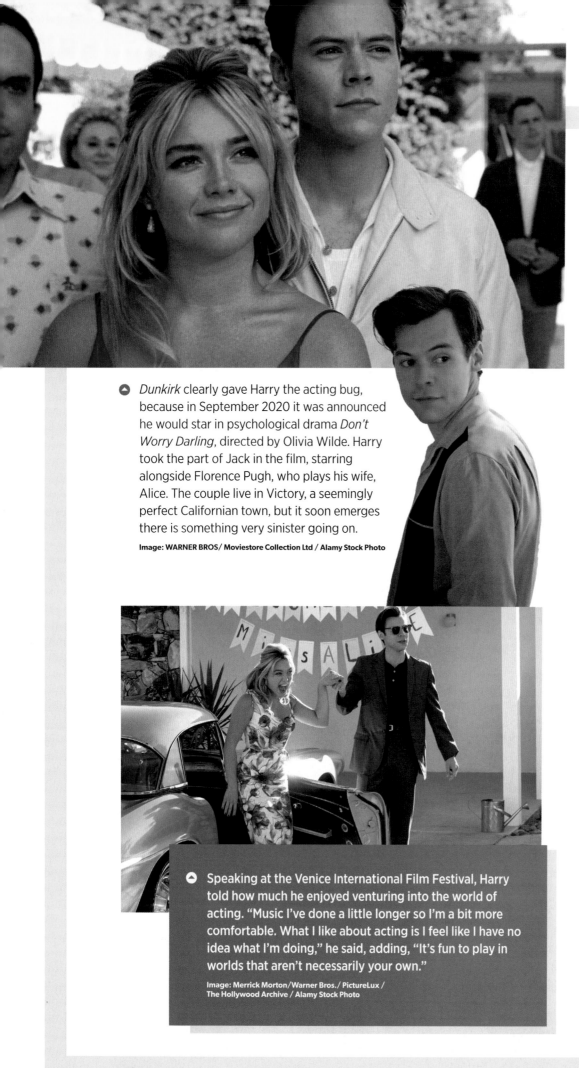

⊙ The film contains steamy scenes between Harry and his on-screen wife, played by Florence Pugh. Talking to Capital Breakfast about *Don't Worry Darling* and his other film, *My Policeman*, Harry even joked, "I don't know that you can watch either with your parents." He added, "I was very lucky to have a very trusting relationship with the people that we were working with, and that kind of came first."

Image: Warner Bros / PictureLux / The Hollywood Archive / Alamy Stock Photo

⊙ *Dunkirk* clearly gave Harry the acting bug, because in September 2020 it was announced he would star in psychological drama *Don't Worry Darling*, directed by Olivia Wilde. Harry took the part of Jack in the film, starring alongside Florence Pugh, who plays his wife, Alice. The couple live in Victory, a seemingly perfect Californian town, but it soon emerges there is something very sinister going on.

Image: WARNER BROS/ Moviestore Collection Ltd / Alamy Stock Photo

⊙ Speaking at the Venice International Film Festival, Harry told how much he enjoyed venturing into the world of acting. "Music I've done a little longer so I'm a bit more comfortable. What I like about acting is I feel like I have no idea what I'm doing," he said, adding, "It's fun to play in worlds that aren't necessarily your own."

Image: Merrick Morton/Warner Bros./ PictureLux / The Hollywood Archive / Alamy Stock Photo

In September, Harry and his co-stars stepped out on the red carpet for the *Don't Worry Darling* premiere, at the Venice International Film Festival. Despite rumours of a feud between Olivia Wilde and Florence Pugh, the cast put on a united front as they posed up a storm. Harry and Olivia – who were then dating – looked incredible in their his and hers Gucci ensembles.

Image: Aurore Marechal/ABACA/ INSTAR Images LLC / Alamy Stock Photo

Did you know?

IT'S BEEN REPORTED THAT HARRY COULD BE IN LINE FOR A FIVE-FILM DEAL WITH MARVEL STUDIOS, RUMOURED TO BE WORTH A WHOPPING $100 MILLION. WHISPERS THAT HE WOULD BE JOINING THE MARVEL CINEMATIC UNIVERSE BEGAN TO CIRCULATE BACK IN 2020, AND WHEN *ETERNALS* WAS RELEASED THE FOLLOWING YEAR, THE MEGASTAR HAD A BRIEF CAMEO AS EROS, THE BROTHER OF VILLAIN THANOS, IN A MID-CREDITS SCENE. ALTHOUGH WE'RE STILL WAITING TO HEAR WHAT HARRY WILL DO NEXT, MARVEL BOSS KEVIN FEIGE HAS SEEMINGLY CONFIRMED THAT HIS CHARACTER WILL RETURN. "THE ADVENTURES OF EROS AND PIP IS SOMETHING THAT IS VERY EXCITING FOR US," HE TOLD MTV NEWS.

Images: Walt Disney Studios Motion Pictures /Marvel Studios /Courtesy Everett Collection /Alamy Stock Photo

Did you know?

HARRY AND DAVID DAWSON SPENT "A GOOD FEW DAYS" REHEARSING FOR THEIR LOVE SCENES. "IT FELT LIKE A BEAUTIFUL DANCE," DAVID SAID. "ME AND HARRY PROMISED EACH OTHER ON DAY ONE THAT WE WOULD ALWAYS LOOK OUT FOR EACH OTHER, THAT WE WOULD ALWAYS CONTINUE TO CHECK IN WITH EACH OTHER. HARRY AND I WANTED THOSE SCENES TO BE THE BEST THEY COULD BE." HARRY ALSO TOLD *THE HOWARD STERN SHOW* THAT HE DID "FEEL VULNERABLE" FILMING THE SCENES, WHICH INVOLVED HIM BEING NAKED. "I'D NEVER KISSED ANYONE ON CAMERA BEFORE AND IT FELT LIKE GIVING A PART OF MYSELF AWAY IN SOME WAYS," HE SAID, ADDING, "I THINK THE MOST IMPORTANT THING IN THAT STUFF IS TRUST."

Images: LANDMARK MEDIA / Alamy Stock Photo

◔ *Don't Worry Darling* and *Dunkirk* aren't Harry's only recent forays into acting. 2022 also saw him star in romantic drama *My Policeman*, which is set in Brighton both in the 1950s and the 1990s. In the poignant film, Harry plays a dashing policeman, Tom Burgess, who dates a teacher called Marion – played by *The Crown*'s Emma Corrin – and teaches her to swim.

Image: LANDMARK MEDIA / Alamy Stock Photo

The pair go on to marry, but while Marion is madly in love with Tom, her new husband is secretly having a love affair with their good friend Patrick, a museum curator played by David Dawson. However, both men are forced to hide their feelings at a time when people were all too often beaten up, arrested and cast out from society for being gay.

Image: LANDMARK MEDIA / Alamy Stock Photo

"It's obviously pretty unfathomable now to think, 'Oh, you couldn't be gay. That was illegal,'" said Harry, in an interview with *Rolling Stone*. "I think everyone, including myself, has your own journey with figuring out sexuality and getting more comfortable with it." He added, "There will be, I would imagine, some people who watch it who were very much alive during this time when it was illegal to be gay."

Image: LANDMARK MEDIA / Alamy Stock Photo

"WE WERE GOING TO THE PONDS AT HAMPSTEAD HEATH IN THE MORNING BEFORE REHEARSALS TO TRY AND ACCLIMATISE OUR BODIES, WHICH WAS QUITE FUNNY"

◀ Emma Corrin called Harry "fantastic to work with," revealing that their filming prep included some chilly swims. "We were told very early on that we had to do some swimming in the sea at Brighton," the star told Virgin Radio. "We were sort of going to the ponds at Hampstead Heath early in the morning before rehearsals. We went there to try and sort of get our bodies acclimatised I guess, which was quite funny."

Image: Brent Perniac/AdMedia
via ZUMA Press Wire/PA Images
Steve Granitz / FilmMagic / Getty Images

IN 2013, ONE DIRECTION RAISED A RECORD-BREAKING £2 MILLION FOR COMIC RELIEF, PARTLY THROUGH THEIR SINGLE 'ONE WAY OR ANOTHER'

In 2013, One Direction raised a record-breaking £2 million for Comic Relief, partly through their single 'One Way Or Another'. The song topped the charts in 63 countries, with the band, Sony and iTunes waiving 100% of the royalties. Harry and the band also made an emotional trip to Ghana, where they met desperately ill children. Back home, Harry also helped create Red Nose Day-themed cakes, to show fans different ways they could fundraise.

Image: Comic Relief/Getty Images

Since his early days in One Direction, kind-hearted Harry has helped raise millions for charitable causes. The band were ambassadors for Rays of Sunshine, a children's charity that grants wishes for seriously ill children. Here they are meeting unwell children ahead of a concert at Wembley Stadium.

Image: Stuart C. Wilson/Getty Images for Rays of Sunshine

▶ Back in 2014, Harry put his ball skills to good use, supporting bandmate Niall Horan's charity football challenge. The singer joined the likes of Olly Murs, Jack Whitehall and James Corden for the match, which saw him scoring a goal. At one point the cheeky star even pulled down rival Piers Morgan's shorts while he watched from the sidelines.

Image: Ben A. Pruchnie/GC Images

Did you know?

In early 2022, Harry pledged to donate at least $1 million of his tour proceeds to gun violence prevention organisation, Everytown. "Along with all of you, I have been absolutely devastated by the recent string of mass shootings in America, culminating at the latest in Robb Elementary School in Uvalde, Texas," he posted on Instagram. "On our North American tour, we will be partnering with Everytown, who work to end gun violence, donating to support their efforts, and sharing their suggested action items. Love, H." The singer also shared the shocking statistic that firearms are the leading cause of death for American children.

IN 2017, HARRY USED HIS VOCAL TALENT TO STAND UP TO CANCER AT THE HOLLYWOOD BOWL, WHEN HE JOINED A STELLAR LINE-UP TO RAISE AWARENESS OF BREAST CANCER

In 2017, Harry used his vocal talent to stand up to cancer at the Hollywood Bowl, when he joined a stellar line-up to raise awareness of breast cancer. He was joined at the We Can Survive concert by Sam Smith, Pink, Lorde and even his ex-bandmate, Niall Horan. Harry sang hits including 'What Makes You Beautiful', and even urged the crowd to sing happy birthday to his mum.

Image: Michael Tran / FilmMagic / Getty Images

STYLE IC

THE REMARKABLE TRANSFORMATION FROM
TEEN CUTIE TO FASHION FRONTMAN

● As early as 2013, Harry began to stand out as the most fashion forward member of One Direction. He quickly moved on from his boyish look in favour of skinny jeans, patterned shirts, snappy jackets, hats and silk scarves. Here he is, looking sharp in a Burberry Prorsum leopard print shirt, navy peak coat, black ripped jeans and Saint Laurent boots.

Image: Gareth Cattermole / Getty Images for Burberry

◀ By the end of 2013, Harry was voted a winner at the British Fashion Awards, fending off competition from the likes of Cara Delevingne and the Duchess of Cambridge. Here he is at the Burberry Prorsum show, during London Fashion Week. Harry joined singer Paloma Faith, actress Sienna Miller and model Suki Waterhouse on the front row.

Image: David M. Benett / Getty Images for Burberry

▶ By 2015, Harry's aesthetic was becoming more flamboyant. While performing with One Direction on *Good Morning America*, he rocked this tiger print silk bomber by Saint Laurent, one of his go-to designers. He cleverly teamed the jacket with black skinny jeans and a black T-shirt, allowing it to take the limelight.

Image: Stephen Lovekin / Getty Images

2017 saw Harry lose his long locks and introduce a series of snappy suits – along with his debut solo album. Here he is arriving at the BBC Radio 1 studios, wearing a red and white chequered suit by British designer Vivienne Westwood. He teamed it with a pair of heeled Gucci loafers, plunging white shirt and simple cross necklace.

Image: Neil Mockford / GC Images

He may have had a number one hit with 'Sign Of The Times' and a starring role in *Dunkirk*, but Harry was determined to make his mark in the fashion world too. From shirts with billowing bows to this incredible red and black Gucci harlequin suit, he repeatedly showed he wasn't afraid to stand out in the style stakes.

Image: David Becker /Getty Images for iHeartMedia

Harry stepped things up a level at the ARIA Awards, when he stormed the stage in this bespoke double-breasted, purple paisley suit. Designed by Alexander McQueen, the jacquard jacket had a shimmering, metallic sheen. Harry expertly completed the look with a pair of copper boxy-toed boots, which were custom-made for the singer by Roker.

Image: Scott Barbour /Getty Images for ARIA

Did you know?

HARRY'S POWDER BLUE SUIT WAS CREATED BY BRITISH DESIGNER CLARE WAIGHT KELLER, AS PART OF HER SPRING 2018 COLLECTION FOR GIVENCHY. THE DESIGNER WOULD HIT THE HEADLINES IN A BIG WAY THE FOLLOWING YEAR WHEN IT EMERGED THAT SHE WAS THE CREATIVE FORCE BEHIND THE DUCHESS OF SUSSEX'S SPECTACULAR WEDDING GOWN. SINGING AT THE VICTORIA'S SECRET FASHION SHOW IN SHANGHAI, CHINA, HARRY TEAMED THE WOOL AND MOHAIR TWO-PIECE WITH A MATCHING SHIRT. AND ALTHOUGH HE WAS SURROUNDED BY LINGERIE-CLAD SUPERMODELS ON THE CATWALK, IT WAS THE POP ICON WHO STOLE THE SHOW.

Images: Taylor Hill / WireImage / Getty

In 2017, Gucci announced that Harry would wear "a selection of one-of-a-kind pieces" designed by creative director Alessandro Michele for his tour that year. And here he is, strutting his stuff on stage at New York's Radio City Music Hall, wearing a custom-made Gucci suit. This time he went for a flocked, floral print – teamed with black heeled loafers. With its slim trousers and sharp tailoring, the outfit evoked a glam rock feel.

Image: Kevin Mazur / Getty Images for Sony Music

Fast-forward to 2018, and Harry is announced as the face of Gucci's new tailoring campaign. In a series of headline-grabbing images he modelled designs by Alessandro Michele, in a St Albans fish and chip shop. Here he is, wearing sliders and a suit with embroidered detail, surrounded by a pack of hungry dogs. The campaign was shot by Glen Luchford and art directed by Christopher Simmonds.

From soft pink trousers to red tuxedo jackets, Harry has rocked a fair few velvet numbers in his time – and this fashion-forward suit was no exception. He donned the electric blue Gucci ensemble to induct singer and friend Stevie Nicks into the Rock & Roll Hall of Fame. He teamed it with a simple white T-shirt, ensuring it was the strokable suit that would do the talking.

Image: Kevin Mazur /Getty Images For The Rock and Roll Hall of Fame

Harry is a mastermind when it comes to accessorising. When he stepped out at the Gucci Cruise fashion show in Italy, he teamed his creamy suit with a pair of rose-tinted sunglasses and black and gold clutch bag. And the attention to detail didn't stop there – he even had his nails painted candy pink and turquoise too.

Image: IPA / WENN Rights Ltd / Alamy Stock Photo

Did you know?

Earlier that year, fans were bemused when snapshots emerged of Harry stroking a rubber chicken while standing on a St Albans street. It soon emerged that he and the hen were both working on the Gucci campaign, which featured feathered friends as well as a pack of adorable dogs. According to reports, Gucci paid the fish and chip shop owner £20,000 a day for the shoot, while local residents were offered up to £100 to move their cars. It's also said that Harry and Gucci donated to local charities, and included local schoolchildren as extras in the shoot.

Image: Suzanne Viner / Retro AdArchives / Alamy Stock Photo

In September 2018, Harry fronted another Gucci campaign, this time posing with pigs and goats instead of chickens and dogs. In the cute shots, taken by photographer Glen Luchford, Harry cuddled up to a piglet in the gardens of an Italian villa. He wore the latest tailoring designs by Alessandro Michele, which included a striking tiger head brooch and vibrant paisley jacket.

Image: Retro AdArchives / Alamy Stock Photo

Harry's style icon status was cemented in 2019, when he co-hosted the Met Gala alongside Lady Gaga, Gucci's Alessandro Michele and *Vogue*'s Anna Wintour. Harry wowed the fashion-focused crowd in Gucci high-waisted, tailored trousers and a sheer, frilled black blouse, teamed with a pair of black patent boots. The elegant look – which revealed his many tattoos – perfectly suited the 'camp' theme of the night.

Image: Karwai Tang / WireImage

Harry's red carpet companion was Gucci's then creative director Alessandro Michele, who helped mastermind the singer's eye-catching look. The pair collaborated with Harry's long-time stylist, Harry Lambert, to create his outfit for the invitation-only event, which features showbiz stars going all-out in outrageous get-ups. Tickets for the do are said to cost over $30,000

Image: James Devaney / GC Images / Getty

Fun Fact

HARRY HAD HIS EARS PIERCED SPECIALLY FOR THE EVENT, WHICH SAW HIM WEARING A SINGLE PEARL DROP EARRING. HIS STYLIST HARRY LAMBERT TOLD MISS VOGUE, "IT WAS THE PERFECT FINAL TOUCH FOR THE OUTFIT. ABOUT FOUR DAYS AGO, THE DAY BEFORE I LEFT TO TRAVEL TO NEW YORK, I WAS ON GUCCI'S WEBSITE AND SAW THESE PEARL EARRINGS." HE ADDED, "HARRY AND I HAVE DISCUSSED PREVIOUSLY PIERCING HIS EARS, AND THIS WAS THE PERFECT TIME. I TEXT HIM AND HE REPLIED, SAYING 'LET'S DO IT'." THE EARRING WASN'T THE ONLY JEWELLERY ROCKED BY HARRY – HIS FINGERS WERE ALSO ADORNED WITH SEVERAL RINGS, INCLUDING A GOLD 'H' AND 'S'.

Image: Theo Wargo / WireImage / Getty

Harry is no stranger to polka dots, and he embraced the look from top-to-toe during this appearance on *The Late Late Show*. With its boxy belted jacket, pocket detail and buttoning, the suit looked like a modern take on safari style. Harry broke up the dotty ensemble – from Gucci's spring/summer 2020 show – with a slender yellow necktie.

Image: Terence Patrick /CBS via Getty Images

Harry has been lauded for dissolving traditional male and female gender norms in fashion, and the 2020 BRIT Awards was a case in point. The singer stole the show in a series of standout looks, starting with this chocolate Gucci suit. Harry teamed it with a lavender knit, lacy collar and pearl necklace, before completing the retro look with a pair of black Mary Jane shoes – adding purple nails to boot.

Image: David M. Benett / Dave Benett / Getty Images

Later that night, Harry dazzled on stage in what would become another iconic look for the star. He donned this spectacular sparkling lace jumpsuit, complete with ivory braces, matching white gloves and of course a single strand of pearls. The precious stones have become something of a signature look for Harry, who has worn them numerous times for photoshoots, stage shows and TV appearances too.

Image: Karwai Tang / WireImage / Getty

Harry's final showstopper that night was this canary yellow Marc Jacobs suit. Never one to do things by halves, the singer paired it with a purple spotty blouse, lavender tulle scarf, white brogues and a smattering of statement rings. Observant fans quickly noticed that they'd seen the three-piece before – Lady Gaga had worn it on the cover of *ELLE* magazine a few months previously.

Image: Richard Young / Shutterstock

Fun Fact

HARRY IS A HUGE FAN OF BEADED NECKLACES, AND MANY OF HIS FAVOURITE STRANDS COME FROM JEWELLERY COMPANY ÉLIOU, WHICH IS THE BRAINCHILD OF DUO CRISTY MANTILLA AND DUDA TEIXEIRA. THE MIAMI-BASED JEWELLERY BRAND SPECIALISES IN HAND-CRAFTED PIECES, MADE USING NATURAL MATERIALS. IN THIS SHOT – TAKEN AT THE SPOTIFY *HARRY'S HOUSE* LISTENING PARTY – THE SINGER IS WEARING THE 'MAZZY' NECKLACE, WHICH SELLS FOR £135 AND IS MADE FROM ACRYLIC BEADS, WITH A GOLD-PLATED CLOSURE. HARRY HAS WORN CUSTOM ÉLIOU NECKLACES AND EVEN COMMISSIONED THE BRAND TO CREATE A LIMITED-EDITION CAPSULE COLLECTION FOR HIS 'MUSIC FOR A SUSHI RESTAURANT' MUSIC VIDEO.

Image: Kevin Mazur / Getty Images for Spotify

Harry once told pal James Corden, "I'm having a year of big pants," and these vibrant, grassy green trousers – which he wore to the SiriusXM Studios in New York – didn't disappoint. He softened the zingy look with a royal blue jumper, pretty scalloped collar and contrasting white boots.

Image: Dia Dipasupil / Getty Images

The 2021 Grammy Awards saw Harry adopt a glam rock look, when he stepped on stage shirtless and wearing a black leather two-piece, designed by Alessandro Michele. The singer added a minty green feather boa, which he slung around his neck and threaded under his cropped jacket. Speaking about the shift in direction, stylist Harry Lambert revealed they wanted to "go for something darker, sexier, and more unexpected."

Image: Anthony Pham via Getty Images

Harry's love of flamboyant suits was back with a bang at the 2021 BRIT Awards. This retro-inspired Gucci number harked back to the 1970s, with its oversized lapels, flared trousers and brazen, psychedelic print. Harry cleverly brought it up to date by teaming it with white trainers and a chocolate brown handbag, with a curved bamboo handle.

Image: JMEnternational / JMEnternational for BRIT Awards / Getty Images

STYLE ICON

This fruity ensemble – worn on *The Howard Stern Show* – perfectly embodies Harry's playful sense of style. He paired the custom Gucci ringer T-shirt with zingy green trousers and a chunky green beaded necklace. It isn't the first time Harry has sizzled in strawberries either – he famously posed in a dress covered by the fruit, designed by Lirika Matoshi.

Image: Cindy Ord / Getty Images for SiriusXM

HARRY FAMOUSLY POSED IN A DRESS DESIGNED BY LIRIKA MATOSHI, WHICH WAS COVERED BY STRAWBERRIES

Harry is famed for his love of all-in-ones, and he certainly shone like a glitter ball in this dazzling jumpsuit while headlining at US music festival, Coachella. The shimmering, sequin-covered costume – which was custom-made by Gucci – proved once again that he's a force to be reckoned with when it comes to all-out, theatrical fashion.

Image: Kevin Mazur / Getty Images Entertainment

In June 2022, it was announced that Gucci's creative director Alessandro Michele and Harry had joined forces to create a collection called Gucci HA HA HA. "Play is at the very heart of the collection," said the design house. "Harry Styles channels his expressive emotionality to play with the meaning of masculinity." Harry showcased some of the impressive new collection at the Venice Film Festival, including these white boots, which have a cheeky red heart detail on the side.

Image: Ernesto Ruscio / Getty Images

Harry wowed at Wembley in June 2022, when he rocked this retro one-piece for the Summertime Ball. Designed by gender neutral clothing line Palomo Spain, the jet-black costume featured sporty white stripes and a belted-waist, while the plunging neckline revealed the singer's striking butterfly and bird tattoos. Harry also wore a simple gold cross around his neck and teamed his bodysuit with black and white trainers.

Image: David Fisher / Global / Shutterstock

Fun Fact

HARRY'S GUCCI COLLECTION WAS NAMED GUCCI HA HA HA BECAUSE THE SINGER AND ALESSANDRO MICHELE HAVE FOR YEARS ENDED THEIR TEXT MESSAGES WITH THE EXPRESSION 'HAHAHA'. HERE IS HARRY, WEARING A CREAM PINSTRIPED JACKET AND BLUE SILK SCARF FROM THE COLLECTION, WHICH IS A COLLABORATION BETWEEN THE LONG-TIME FRIENDS. THE SINGER-TURNED-MOVIE STAR STEPPED OUT IN THE ELEGANT LOOK IN VENICE, ITALY, AT THE PHOTOCALL FOR HIS FILM *DON'T WORRY DARLING*. HARRY, WHO ARRIVED BY WATER TAXI, TEAMED THE OVERSIZED JACKET WITH NAVY FLARED TROUSERS, TINTED SHADES AND BROWN TASSELLED GUCCI LOAFERS. HE ADDED A FISTFUL OF RINGS FOR GOOD MEASURE, AND A SIMPLE WHITE VEST.

Image: Stephane Cardinale / Corbis via Getty Images

⬆ Harry stepped things up another notch with this custom JW Anderson jumpsuit, which he wore while performing on the *Today* show at the Rockefeller Plaza. With its flared sleeves and zany stripes, the look certainly made a style statement – and went down a storm with fans. The all-in-one was based on a dress from the British brand's Resort 2022 collection.

Image: Gilbert Carrasquillo / GC Images / Getty

FRIENDS & FAMILY

MEET THE HEART-THROB'S NEAREST AND DEAREST WHO HAVE SUPPORTED HIM EVERY STEP OF THE WAY

Fun Fact

WHEN ONE DIRECTION FIRST STARTED OUT, THE BAND WOULD CONGREGATE AT JAMES CORDEN'S HOUSE FOR PIZZA AND GAMES ON THE PLAYSTATION. HARRY HAS NOW BEEN FRIENDS WITH THE TV HOST FOR YEARS, AND THEY'VE EVEN HOLIDAYED TOGETHER – THEY FLEW TO THE CARIBBEAN IN 2019, TO SEE IN THE NEW YEAR. OF COURSE, HARRY HAS ALSO APPEARED ON *THE LATE LATE SHOW* MULTIPLE TIMES, ACTING IN HILARIOUS SKITS WITH HIS PAL. "OUR FRIENDSHIP HAS GROWN, AND I LOVE HIM VERY, VERY MUCH," SAID JAMES. "I'M VERY PROUD OF HIM AND PROTECTIVE OF HIM, ALWAYS."

Image: Terence Patrick / CBS via Getty Images

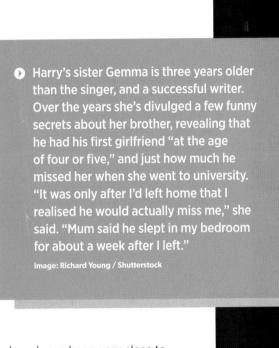

> Harry's sister Gemma is three years older than the singer, and a successful writer. Over the years she's divulged a few funny secrets about her brother, revealing that he had his first girlfriend "at the age of four or five," and just how much he missed her when she went to university. "It was only after I'd left home that I realised he would actually miss me," she said. "Mum said he slept in my bedroom for about a week after I left."

Image: Richard Young / Shutterstock

◀ Harry has always been very close to his mum, Anne, who has been spotted holidaying with the star and enjoying his Love On Tour concerts. The singer even played best man in 2013, when she wed her long-time partner, Robin Twist, who helped bring up Harry after his parents separated. Despite his fame, Harry said his speech was "the most nerve-wracking thing" he had ever done. Sadly, Robin passed away in 2017, after a battle with cancer.

Image: Richard Young / Shutterstock

◀ The One Direction boys might not get together as often as they'd like, but Harry recently revealed they have a "deep love" for one another. In an interview with Zane Lowe, for Apple, he chatted about their experience in the band, saying, "I feel like there's very much a respect between all of us. We did something together and that is something that you can't really undo. It's a very deep love for each other, I think."

Image: Stuart C. Wilson / Getty Images for Rays of Sunshine

Harry worked with director Olivia Wilde on her film *Don't Worry Darling*, and their romance went public in January 2021. Although they've kept their relationship low key, Olivia has praised Harry for his "talent", "humility" and "grace", saying, "To me, he's very modern and I hope that this brand of confidence as a male that Harry has – truly devoid of any traces of toxic masculinity – is indicative of his generation and therefore the future of the world."

Image: Neil Mockford / GC Images

It was recently reported that the couple were taking a break from their romance, due to their hectic schedules. While Harry's tour will be taking him abroad to South America, Australia, Asia and Europe, Olivia's work and children are based in Los Angeles. She is mum to Otis, eight, and Daisy, six, from her previous relationship with actor Jason Sudeikis.

Image: Kevin Mazur / WireImage / Getty images

THE PAIR ARE RUMOURED TO HAVE DATED ON AND OFF

Kendall Jenner is an old pal of Harry's, but the pair are also rumoured to have dated on and off when they were younger. Any romance clearly hasn't affected their friendship though – the model was spotted dancing at one of Harry's concerts in November 2022, alongside her sister Kylie Jenner and friend Hailey Bieber.

Image: Kevin Mazur / MG19 / Getty Images for The Met Museum / Vogue

Harry briefly dated Taylor Swift in 2012, but the pictures of the pair on a date in Central Park sparked a media frenzy. And five years later, Harry admitted that navigating the scrutiny had been tough. "Relationships are hard, at any age," he told *Rolling Stone*. "And adding in that you don't really understand exactly how it works when you're 18, trying to navigate all that stuff didn't make it easier," he said. "It was a learning experience for sure."

Image: David Krieger / GC Images / Getty images

HARRY REPORTEDLY EXPLORED THE BREAK UP WITH CAMILLE IN HIS SONG 'CHERRY' AND EVEN FEATURES HER VOICE AT THE END OF THE TRACK

In 2017, Harry started dating French model Camille Rowe. But the pair ended the relationship a year later, and Harry reportedly explored the break up in his song 'Cherry'. "I was feeling not great. It's all about being not great," he told Zane Lowe. Harry, who is thought to have stayed friends with Camille, even features her voice at the end of the track.

Image: JB Lacroix / WireImage / Getty

Did you know?

Ex-Radio 1 DJ Nick Grimshaw has been buddies with Harry right from his early days in the limelight, and the pair once famously went live on air together having partied all night at the BRIT Awards. When Nick left the station Harry recorded a sweet tribute, saying, "My favourite time being on Radio 1 with you was probably forming the Straight Through Crew and going straight in from the BRITs." He added, "Thank you for being a friend and I miss you and I can't wait to see you soon. Good luck with everything, I love you. Byeeee!"

Image: Dave M. Benett / Getty Images

◀ Pals Harry and Lizzo brought the house down with their duet at Coachella, and just three months later the singer sent her a gorgeous bunch of orange, pink and yellow flowers to celebrate the success of her hit, 'About Damn Time'. "Yall harry got me flowers congratulating me on about damn time going #1," she revealed on TikTok. "Thanks for the flowers, Harry."

Image: JM Enternational / Shutterstock

Harry is a huge fan of Stevie Nicks and in 2015 he gave her a carrot cake for her birthday, after a Fleetwood Mac concert. The thoughtful gesture sparked a great friendship, even leading to a co-performance, and Harry later called her, "everything you've ever wanted in a lady, a lover, in a friend." Stevie who's 72, has spoken glowingly in return, calling Harry "the son I never had."

Image: Kevin Mazur / Getty Images For The Rock and Roll Hall of Fame

STEVIE HAS SPOKEN GLOWINGLY ABOUT HARRY, CALLING HIM "THE SON I NEVER HAD"

Did you know?

HARRY AND LOUIS TOMLINSON WERE ALWAYS FIRM FRIENDS, BUT FALSE RUMOURS THAT THE PAIR WERE HAVING A RELATIONSHIP CAUSED DISTANCE BETWEEN THEM DURING ONE DIRECTION. "IT CREATED THIS ATMOSPHERE BETWEEN THE TWO OF US WHERE EVERYONE WAS LOOKING INTO EVERYTHING WE DID," EXPLAINED LOUIS. THANKFULLY THOUGH, IT SEEMS THEY'VE PUT ANY AWKWARDNESS BEHIND THEM. "I LOOK ON HARRY LIKE A BROTHER, MAN," LOUIS SAID RECENTLY. "I HAVE A LOT OF PRIDE FOR WHAT HE'S DOING." SPEAKING OF THE BAND, HE ADDED, "WE CHECK IN ON EACH OTHER, WE'RE GOOD LIKE THAT."

Images: Astrid Stawiarz / Getty Images

⏶ Harry has been buddies with popstar Ed Sheeran for years and the pair once even visited a tattoo parlour together, to have what Harry has dubbed a "bro tat". The pair opted for *Pingu* inkings, in homage to the TV show, which was a firm favourite with both singers growing up. While Harry has the name Pingu inked under his arm, Ed has the cartoon character on his upper left arm.

Image: Kevin Mazur / Fox / WireImage

Celebrate the songs and sounds of the greatest decades in music

Explore the lives and legacies of some of the world's most iconic artists

Crank up the volume and get to know the best rock and metal bands on the planet

Get great savings when you buy direct from us

1000s of great titles, many not available anywhere else

World-wide delivery and super-safe ordering

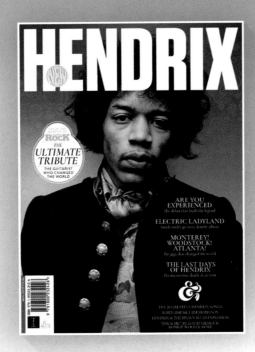

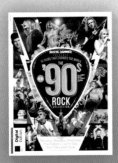

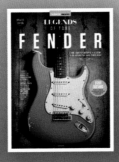